Praise fo

This book will add value to a vet's plan for transition from the military or a deployment back into "The World." There are many options for military personnel who are returning from war or transitioning to civilian life, some excellent, some horrible, and many in between. You are on point when you say that veterans should feed the core strength built or reinforced by military service, and leverage it into the workforce. You built the core strengths into a strategic option toward an exceptional future for a trooper who wants that."

– Colonel William L. Peace, Army National Guard

The Empowered Veteran shines a light on those unshakable attributes that differentiate veterans as the force multiplier they are in our economy and communities. Hiring managers and investors need to read this book, too; it will help them become familiar with our core strengths. I wish I had this resource when I transitioned from the Army. Thank you, Dwayne, for your exceptional commitment to our brothers and sisters.

– Marjorie K. Eastman, Army veteran, award-winning author, *The Frontline Generation*

Dwayne Paro has put together a straightforward plan of action for transitioning service members and veterans. Read and implement the strategies covered in this book and become empowered to master your transition and life.

– Andrew Marr, Green Beret, co-founder of Warrior Angels Foundation, co-host of *The Warrior Soul* podcast

The Empowered Veteran is the shortcut for those at the earliest stages of transitioning out of service and a lifesaver to those exiting under a more short suspense. The programs in place across the branches still follow a curriculum formed like it's the late 1990s or early 2000s. Dwayne masterfully identifies the white space for today's exiting service members by suffocating the BS and outdated tactics to provide practical guidance for the next wave of battle-ready civilians in the workplace and on the entrepreneur front.

– Doc Collins, former Army combat medic, founder of Patriot Heart Press, author, speaker

The Empowered Veteran is a magnificent book – a fabulous resource for veterans, enlisted military, and champions of veterans. Dwayne Paro created a comprehensive gem that will have a significant and very positive impact on the lives of our beloved vets. It is a real bonus that *The Empowered Veteran* includes an exceptional workbook that will empower our vets to embrace the tremendous wisdom they gain and take it to an immediate state of action. *The Empowered Veteran* is a must-read for vets – and for all of us because we owe them everything. This is a real masterpiece.

– Chrissy Carew, master certified coach, *The Insightful Player*

Sharing personal challenges and defeats are not easy. Sharing challenges and failures to help others is audacious and noble. Dwayne shared his challenges and the lessons he learned on his journey. Dwayne is a veteran who understands other veterans. *The Empowered Veteran* addresses topics that the majority of veterans do not want to discuss. Dwayne doesn't allow veterans to hide, and he breaks the silence by offering to be the first person to share personal experiences.

– Michael Barbera, consumer psychologist, CEO, Barbera Solutions

The Empowered Veteran is a must-read for all veterans; especially those who are in the transitioning process. Dwayne synthesizes his military service and his professional experiences into an easy-to-read handbook that delivers actionable guidance. This book should be in the hands of all transitioning service members no later than twelve months from their date of separation. True empowerment stems from knowledge – this book is the knowledge you need before beginning your next career. Personally and professionally, I am proud to provide *The Empowered Veteran* my recommendation.

– Corey M Christman, special agent (ret) USAF, CEO, Vethos, LLC

One of the best pieces of advice I could give a transitioning veteran is to use your resources. You don't have to try to figure everything out on your own. *The Empowered Veteran* is a compass. It is a powerful resource for transitioning veterans (and those who may have not quite found their way yet). Dwayne has done a great job assembling a framework to help veterans find their way. The book coaches veterans on how to identify and leverage the core strengths they honed in the military. It also provides a roadmap that helps them figure out how to get where they want to be. Use this book to shoot an azimuth and be aware of the terrain ahead.

– Nick Bradfield, Marine veteran and entrepreneur

The Empowered Veteran is a must for any transitioning veteran. The book is easy to read and reaches you on a personal level as if Dwayne is talking to you one on one. The option to interact with the book via workbook sections allows for a more personal connectedness to the information. Being a combat veteran myself, I wish I had this book when I transitioned back into civilian life, but it is still a valuable handbook for my life today. I genuinely believe this is a handbook for life and personal growth that every transitioning veteran should carry on their person.

– Christopher "Sarge" Carlson, Army veteran, *Sarge Approved* podcast

Way to go Dwayne. Thanks for putting together another great resource for not only our fellow veterans but also those active duty soldiers, sailors, airmen, and marines soon to re-enter the civilian ranks!

– Jon Taylor, Navy veteran,
founder of MrQuickPick USA

Dwayne is a caring, intelligent, force for good. He is just the guy to write a book entitled *The Empowered Veteran* because he encourages that empowerment every day.

– Rick Yost, veteran, CEO of Veteranslist

This book nails it by encouraging transitioning service members to be curious and "seek knowledge." Dwayne points out clearly with the "No excuses" commentary that you are in an enviable position most civilian won't find: you as a veteran have military discipline and a GI Bill at your disposal. My God! What an advantage that is! Complete all your tasks in life and move on; you will be a better person for that commitment in yourself. I love that Dwayne included some great quotes at the end; I draw great motivation and cover from quotes that I apply to my "vetrepreneur" enterprise. This book is a great reminder for me personally to constantly seek knowledge. Thank you for your service, discipline, and a great read Mr. Paro!

– Joe Meisch, Army veteran, CEO and
founder of Temple Massager

I've read dozens of books, articles, and reports about and for transitioning veterans. As a service member, I went through the Navy's transition assistance program. Dwayne's approach to inventorying your skills is like no other. He gets to the crux of what civilian employers need, but more importantly what will drive you to ever-greater levels of success.

Also, drawing from his own experience as a transitioning veteran and his keen insight into the pitfalls of reintegration,

Dwayne offers sage advice. With *The Empowered Veteran* in hand, you can avoid many stumbling blocks to success that have hampered too many service members.

Bravo Zulu Dwayne on creating a resource for reintegration that's relevant to the 21st-century veteran.

**– LCDR Kevin Bemel, Command Chaplain,
Navy Warrior Transition Program – Sembach and author
of *The 8 Deadly Sins of Job-Hunting – Veterans' Edition***

THE EMPOWERED VETERAN

STRENGTH AND CONFIDENCE TO HARNESS YOUR FUTURE

DWAYNE D. PARO

ISBN: 978-1-944878-78-8

DEDICATION

This book is dedicated to all the service men and women who have selflessly sacrificed for our great nation. There is no greater honor than to voluntarily serve your nation with no expectation of return, other than knowing you are equipped for any challenge life may bring.

As a fellow veteran, I offer this guide to support you in creating the empowering and fulfilling future you desire and deserve. The information in this book has been garnered from my personal and professional experience, coaching clients, interviewing veterans for my podcast, and many conversations with veterans in different stages and situations of a transition. I hope you find this book useful and empowering to your transition and future.

This is a special dedication to my grandfather, Wilfred Paro, and my father, David Paro, for their combat service and to my brother Derrick Paro for his military service to our great nation.

TABLE OF CONTENTS

FOREWORD

Going from one chapter in life to the next can be hard, whether it's moving to a new school, a new job, or a new relationship. When it comes to transitioning from the military to civilian culture, it can feel like you're moving to a foreign country. You must make new friends, learn a new lingo, and change your lifestyle—and very few people around you will understand what you are going through.

The military offers documented and standardized paths to achieve success, such as standard operating procedures, technical manuals, and professional training schools. However, when it comes to leaving the military and transitioning into civilian life, there are very few resources that help a veterans translate their military success and knowledge into something compatible for their new environment. *The Empowered Veteran* is that resource.

When I left drill sergeant duty for the civilian world, I had an office job for about six weeks before I was fired. The issue wasn't my work ethic, but my difficulty assimilating to the new culture around me. I failed again when I attempted to become a police officer, something that I felt would be an easy transition with my military background. I performed above average in their tests and performance evaluations, but I was rejected because of their concern that I wouldn't fit in. They probably were right, because I wasn't ready.

I didn't have a resource like *The Empowered Veteran* to explain the key differences in cultures and expectations that must be understood as early in the transition process as possible. While various federal agencies offer transition assistance programs that provide generic support, these programs are costly for the government to run and are not properly resourced. Most transitioning military members find they need more support to make a successful transition. I relied solely on what the government provided, and it was not adequate.

That's why this book, *The Empowered Veteran*, is of great value. It's like the advanced course to those programs: a resource veterans can rely on, once the class is over, that teaches how to approach and navigate successfully through their transition.

While my transition was not easy, I did find great success through entrepreneurship when I started Grunt Style. I created the company based on the military structure and the pride and patriotism that I found within it. I knew that this was something I wanted to share with the rest of the country. The road was definitely not easy, and there was no map or set of directions to lead me to success; I had to pave those paths myself.

Dwayne's great success in climbing the corporate ladder to the top as an executive qualifies him to write *The Empowered Veteran*. As you will see, he has brilliantly highlighted the challenges he faced along the way and was able to overcome using the strategies and strengths he shares. When I'm staffing my company, I look for the strengths and experiences Dwayne outlines. You can be successful in your transition—whether it is working for a company, becoming an entrepreneur, or some combination of the two—if you apply the focus that is outlined within this book.

To be successful, you need a plan. It doesn't matter who or what it is—planning can be the difference between success and failure. Dwayne has spelled out how to develop the various plans needed and the reasoning behind them.

Be prepared to invest in yourself and do so in a methodical and systematic approach. Trying to do it all at once or too much at a time can be overwhelming; prioritize based on what will add the most value at the stage of transition you are in.

You must commit to success to achieve it. You must be willing and able to allow for self-reflection and critique to foster personal and business growth.

Get started—and good luck!

- Dan Alarik,
Founder and CEO of Grunt Style

INTRODUCTION

We all have a story, a path we've been on, and ultimately a place we are going. At times, we will find ourselves at a crossroads; this may seem like we are lost, unsure of what's next, or just trying to decide to commit long-term to something we are passionate about. No matter where you are or where you've been, there is a future for you and a path to get there. With the amazing core strengths engrained in you from your time in the military, whether that is two years or twenty, you have what it takes to be successful during and after a transition.

I've been able to use my core strengths to pivot at the right times so that I'm not reinventing myself and throwing away what I have accomplished to do something different. You can, too. This book will show you how.

You don't have to have any particular background or experience to apply the concepts I discuss in this book. All veterans have similar core strengths that can and must be leveraged to establish fulfilling futures that are empowering for them and their families.

I've been told I have an "inspiring and empowering story that needs to be told." I'm going to share personal life examples throughout this book to illustrate my points. Of course, your experience will be unique. My intent is not to pat myself on the back or try to convince someone I had it better or worse than them. My mission – and my passion – is to support veterans in transition, and real-world examples are a great way to do this.

I ask that as you review this material, you bring a positive approach and an open mind. When you can understand what might be another frame of reference, this book will have incredible value as you transition into a civilian career. Just take what works for you and apply it.

Let me share my background with you so you can appreciate my passion for supporting veterans and start to trust, know, and connect with me as a guide on your journey.

Early in my life, I decided to follow in my ancestors' footsteps and join the military. I always felt a calling to serve my country and others. My family has generations of combat veterans dating back to World War II and possibly before. I served in the Air Force from 1991 to 1999. My first assignment was to Rome Laboratory in Rome, New York. In 1994, I was selected for a tour overseas to support Operation Southern Watch in Saudi Arabia as part of Operation Desert Storm/Shield.

While serving in theater, I sustained a life-threatening injury at the Operations and Maintenance Squadron, where I was assigned. The fact that I survived was my first inclination that I had a higher life purpose.

I finished my time on active duty in a special duty assignment to the Pentagon. I then transitioned to the Air Force Reserve and Air National Guard.

I chose to pursue a life ambition in the Information Technology field. Over the next two decades, I earned advanced degrees and certifications, which helped propel me to an executive position. While this was a pinnacle achievement in my career and it provided very well for my family, I was missing something in the nature of service, a desire which is at my core. I was no longer serving something of greater importance like I did in the military.

September 11, 2001, offered another nudge that perhaps it was time for me to pursue a life of greater purpose versus ambition. I was scheduled to be at the Pentagon that day, but I postponed the appointment because another client needed me.

The plane slammed into the first floor of the Pentagon, directly below the computer system I was to be working on that day. I later saw a picture showing the roof of the Pentagon leaning on the rack of that computer system and four crumbled floors below.

I spent many weeks working with the charred remains of the system the FBI recovered from the building. The smell of burnt jet fuel on the equipment shook me to my core. This led to several years of deep inner reflection and analysis to find ways to serve others and create a future that included living my life's purpose. During this time, I spent several years working on the Combatting Terrorism teams for the Defense Intelligence Agency and Federal Bureau of Investigation, receiving a continuous excellence award for my efforts. These assignments brought me back to living for a greater purpose because I was able to work to combat terrorism and implement the core strengths I developed in the military. After completing this important and fulfilling role, I returned to pursue my ambition of working as an IT executive, This field utilized my core strengths, including my technical skills and intelligence, but I continued to feel unfulfilled in my daily pursuits.

After more deep reflection, it became self-evident that I didn't want another J.O.B. I wanted fulfilling work that was more of a lifestyle pursuit. Eventually, I came across the field of coaching.

I am known and well respected for my personable leadership style and for partnering with others who want to grow in their personal and professional lives. Coaching utilized my greatest strength and value: the natural ability and passion for serving others and supporting them as they expand their lives and careers. It became apparent that this is my life purpose. Through deeper reflection and self-study, I realized I was prepared to pursue my passion, which used all of my life experiences up to that point.

As I established my veteran empowerment and transition practice, putting in motion my life purpose, I have experienced validation and various synchronicities that have confirmed this is the right path for me. As I continue to find avenues to add value to the transitioning veteran population, I have established a very honorable and impressive network with others who are also living their life purpose to serve our transitioning veterans. I am also honored to showcase combat veterans who have become successful entrepreneurs on my *Charlie Mike* podcast.

As you read this book, I hope you can relate to the core strengths I've identified and find ways to apply them to create the future you desire and deserve. Answering the questions posed throughout the book will allow you to build a repertoire of information you can use to define and move forward with your amazing future.

Please let me know how this book has impacted you and supported you as you transition from active duty to civilian life. I'd love to learn your story and maybe even share it on my website and with my clients.

Dwayne Paro
Veteran Empowerment and Transition Coach

Part I

Ready – Leverage Your Core Strengths

Certain core strengths will significantly increase your chances of living a purpose-driven and rewarding life. The military has identified these core strengths and has integrated them into the training of every member of the Armed Forces. These strengths become evident when you are in the presence of a veteran. Once you have been through training in any of the branches of service, you are endowed with these core strengths for the rest of your life, no matter how long you served this great nation. You need only believe in them and practice them as part of your daily life.

I've had the honor of interviewing numerous transitioning veterans and many who have been out of military service for years. In each of these in-depth conversations, I found a common theme arises no matter what else is discussed. These veterans shared what I refer to as proven core strengths they gained in their military service:

- Perseverance: Accomplish the task at hand no matter what, no excuses
- Accountability and Dependability: Consistently meet the mission requirements
- Thirst for Knowledge: Quick and adept learner
- Commitment to Excellence: Evolving aptitude
- Caring Leader: Knowing when to lead and when to follow
- Integrity: Commitment to humility and being a team player
- Ability to Influence: Understanding what others need and providing service and support that benefits both sides
- Understanding the Use of Emotional Intelligence: Ability to effectively manage emotions and interpersonal relationships
- Effective Communication: Build and sustain rapport with all personality styles and ranks
- Displaying Adaptability: Be open and respectful of other people's ideas and capabilities
- Success in Stressful Situations: Knowing that you have endured and succeeded in similar high-stress situations
- Embrace Lifelong Learning: Quickly grasping new technical and leadership knowledge
- Being an Immediate Contributor: Proactively positioning yourself to be ready when needed

Several other core strengths have been key to transitioning veterans' successes, but these are the ones I have found to be consistently common among veterans.

"Connect to your core, and you'll find strength. Act from your core, and you'll move mountains."

– Gabriella Goddard

Can you identify any additional core strengths you have acquired through being in the military?

____

____

____

____

____

PERSEVERANCE: ACCOMPLISH THE TASK AT HAND NO MATTER WHAT, NO EXCUSES

"Many of life's failures are people who did not realize how close they were to success when they gave up."

– Thomas Edison

Service members are trained with the fortitude to push through even the toughest of situations, making this strength a part of the very fabric of their being. Your mindset will greatly influence your ability to persevere in tough conditions even after you have left the military. If you embody the notion that things will be tough, but manageable, you can achieve anything.

As a world-class endurance athlete and coach, Christopher Bergland should know about the power of perseverance: "Dopamine is the fuel that keeps people motivated to persevere and achieve a goal,"

Bergland wrote in *Psychology Today*. "You have the power to increase your production of dopamine by changing your attitude and behavior. Scientists have identified higher levels of dopamine—also known as the 'reward molecule'—as being linked to forming lifelong habits, such as perseverance."

A great aspect of the military is that it is a no-excuses environment, which is heightened during times of conflict. Lives depend on accomplishing the task at hand, no matter what. There will be many challenges that will be faced in your day-to-day life as you work toward reaching your personal vision. These problems must be overcome, and the core strength to do that is perseverance. You may have in your mind the perfect timeframe or outcome, but many times that is not what happens. As long as you keep pushing forward and don't allow yourself to be drawn down by the obstacles in your way, you will accomplish your goals to reach your vision.

The definition of perseverance is the steadfastness in doing something despite difficulty or delay in achieving success.

If you know that there will be difficulty and/or delay in the process, you can plan for this and not be surprised when it happens or let it distract or derail you.

Persevering by leveraging those obstacles will be key. Many situations in life will push people to their limits and beyond. These experiences build us into who we are, and if used properly, can set us up for great success.

In the introduction, I shared that I sustained a life-threatening injury while deployed to Saudi Arabia. A misdiagnosis from the medical staff led to numerous complications over time, and unfortunately, in this type of environment, there is no such thing as a sick day. For many days, I had to persevere through the significant lack of sleep and pain I was experiencing. Simple tasks were difficult to handle, and the more complex tasks and responsibilities were near impossible to focus on. But for the safety of myself and those around me in this environment, I had to do all I could every day to persevere through the situation. On many days I could have just given up and given in to the infection and blood clot forming in my head, which quickly would have overcome my ability to survive. Fortunately for me, the support of others concerned about my condition—and my perseverance—enabled me to survive the situation.

There are many benefits to having perseverance as a core strength:

- Others notice, and you are seen as a role model.
- It builds the internal character that will serve you well in many situations.
- You build a repertoire of tough situations with positive outcomes to look back on for future challenges.
- Your confidence continues to increase, knowing you have faced similar and even more significant challenges.

My favorite statement when I face challenges and obstacles is *"No Matter What!"* I will persevere no matter what obstacle is in front of me and no matter what others say or do.

"Creating a steady flow of dopamine is fundamental to creating a habit of perseverance," writes Bergland. "This incredible neurochemical is accessible to everyone. YOU have the power to tap into your internal dopamine reserves on demand. Learning and conditioning yourself to self-administer this 'reward molecule' every day can turn anyone into a go-getter. With a slight attitude adjustment and a shift in perspective, everybody has the power to become more perseverant by tapping the universal power of dopamine. The ability to create a habit of perseverance isn't something reserved for a few—it is available to you!"

You can tap into that dopamine reserve by maintaining a positive mindset. Dr. Barbara Fredrickson notes in her "broaden and build" theory that a positive attitude keeps you open to all your options. It increases your optimism and your dopamine levels. Research by Dr. William Larkin and Dr. Donald Johnson of the Applied Neuroscience Institute has found similar results.

In what ways have you modeled perseverance in your life? Use this list for future reference when things get tough.

____

____

____

____

____

ACCOUNTABILITY/ DEPENDABILITY: CONSISTENTLY MEET THE MISSION REQUIREMENTS

"Accountability it is not only what we do, but also what we do not do, for which we are accountable."

– Moliere

You are there to support the mission. This drives everything that matters in the space where you are working. The military trains and executes based on mission. Without a mission, how do you know where you are going and what needs to be done? In the military, lives depend on properly executing the mission *down to the letter*. Therefore, those supporting the mission must be accountable and dependable at all times.

Accountability is the fact or condition of being responsible. Dependability is the quality of being able to be counted on or relied upon.

In the most extreme situations, such as when our special forces go in to capture a known terrorist, you can imagine that they have planned, written, and practiced the execution of the mission many times over. They know going into a situation what's right and what's not right, so they have decision points to press on or abort. This level of accountability should be no different in the civilian sector. Every organization has a mission, and the employees must be accountable for their actions and depended on to get their role accomplished. It becomes quickly apparent when someone is not performing their role. This could be for any one of the following reasons:

- The project is costing more than planned.
- The project is off schedule.
- There are unintended breaks in the process.
- People don't show up on time.
- They don't put in the extra effort required to overcome the unanticipated obstacles.

There are many benefits to maintaining accountability and dependability as a core strength:

- You are seen as a leader.
- You raise the team to a new level.
- The respect you garner will earn promotions and rewards.
- Your reputation will precede you in performing various missions.
- You become the go-to person when someone needs to ensure their mission will be completed.

Over the years, I have become an expert in taking over programs that are not going well. I was brought into a $30 million information technology project for a federal client because they were over budget, behind schedule, and understaffed. The government had issued a "get well" letter to our corporate office stating that if we could not bring the contract up to standards, we would lose the work. Going into these situations is never easy, but with my military background and accountability and dependability among my core strengths, I'm able to persevere. After nine long months of days averaging over twelve hours and working up to six days a week, we saved the contract. We found cost savings to bring the budget back in line, figured out how to get back on schedule (and eventually ahead of schedule), and fully staffed the contract. None of this would have been possible without having personal accountability and being dependable to get the mission done.

Someone is always watching and expecting that those who wore the uniform of this great nation have something that others do not. You can be the model and leader who shows that these core strengths are part of who you are and that you are the one they need.

How do others view your level of accountability and why?

____

____

____

____

How do others view your level of dependability and why?

____

____

____

____

____

What are some examples of how your accountability and dependability could be used to define the value you can add to an organization?

____

____

____

____

____

THIRST FOR KNOWLEDGE: QUICK AND ADEPT LEARNER

"It is possible to fly without motors, but not without knowledge and skill."

– Wilbur Wright

Obtaining a formal education beyond high school has become a must for those who want to build a solid career in the civilian sector. There was a time when this was not the case. You could graduate from high school, spend time in the military, separate, and be able to find a meaningful job that would allow you to live a comfortable life based on the skills you obtained while serving our country.

Most all job postings will have some formal education requirement. This is not only for senior-level employees but for those just starting out. Employers see a formal education as a sign of what someone is willing to do to succeed and progress in their careers, and that they take selfless time and focus outside of work to achieve it. A degree shows that you are self-driven, you have a sincere desire to succeed in your pursuits, and what you will be able to do for the organization. It also shows you have a certain level of knowledge that another individual may not be able to obtain quickly enough or through their existing experiences.

The military teaches members to learn new skills or procedures quickly and have the desire to continue to grow in knowledge. This is a highly desirable skill in the civilian sector, as change is the norm and is constant. Depending on the industry, it's more frequent and rapid, which can be challenging to those not used to being able to pick up on new knowledge and information quickly.

Being a quick and adept learner will provide many benefits as you move forward:

- Potential employers will see this as a strength.
- Your confidence in your pursuits will increase.
- You will always be preparing for your future.
- You will enrich the lives of those around you.
- More significant opportunities will be available to you.

Thirst for knowledge combined with being a quick and adept learner is a core strength that is important to integrate. Your transition from the military will be more successful if your education aligns with your career aspirations.

The cost of a formal education often prohibits people from getting the knowledge they need to further their career. You are fortunate to have extraordinary benefits to support your education goals before you leave the service.

While you are in the military, take advantage of the educational opportunities that will position you for your future endeavors. Using your education benefits to get as much education as possible will pay off big when you transition. I took advantage of my GI Bill to get my bachelor's degree while I was in the military. Without a lot of senior-level experience, this gave me a leg up in securing a great position before transitioning out. That bachelor's degree served me for several years working in the industry. Eventually, I needed a master's degree to obtain an executive level position. The company I worked for paid for its employees' tuition for advanced degrees in exchange for a two-year commitment upon completion of the degree. For me, that was a huge gift and an easy decision as I was used to signing up for four-year commitments in the military. My advice is to find those organizations that make education for their employees a priority and be in a position to leverage that benefit.

Being self-driven in obtaining knowledge outside of formal education is important as well. I read at least two to three books a month that vary in topic but are providing me insight into what I can do to grow in my life. This is all part of having an insatiable thirst for knowledge!

Is your current level of education sufficient to progress in your career? If not, what are a couple actions (with timelines) you will commit to taking so that it can be?

____

____

____

____

____

COMMITMENT TO EXCELLENCE: EVOLVING APTITUDE

"Striving for excellence motivates you; striving for perfection is demoralizing."

– Harriet Braiker

We should all strive for excellence. This doesn't in any way mean perfection, which in my opinion is unattainable, as there is always room for improvement and things evolve over time. Striving for excellence is all about evolving your aptitude. You should constantly be looking to take on new skills and knowledge in anything that you are a part of. This will allow you to grow over time and increase the level of complexity and sophistication that you can take on for an organization.

You must be able to step back and assess your present aptitude in areas of importance to your future success. Being self-critical is important; you want to position yourself to improve any areas that are lacking. This may require that you ask a trusted source who knows you well to make the same type of assessment. Between the two assessments is a happy medium indicating where you should put your focus for committing to excellence.

The military believes firmly in this core strength, as it is imperative that we stay ahead of our adversaries and that those who are serving in the military are ready at a moment's notice to answer the call of defending our freedoms.

There are many benefits to having a commitment to excellence as a core strength:

- You are always working on improving your aptitude.
- You are a role model for those around you.
- It positions you for greater opportunity.
- The organizations you are part of are better off.

I had the honor of serving on the Defense Intelligence Agency combatting terrorism team after 9/11. I was a federal contractor brought in to stand up and manage the IT infrastructure that the analysts would use to do their critical work. This was a very stressful environment with long days that led into each other. However, due to the mission we were charged with, these obstacles were of no importance. I spent six years on this team and was presented an award of Continuous Excellence when I left for the Federal Bureau of Investigation's Combatting Terrorism team. Of all the awards I've ever received, this one has the most value, not only because of the mission but because I was personally able to sustain a level of excellence in one of the most challenging environments I've ever worked in. My aptitude certainly far exceeded my expectations in growth over the many years supporting this mission. I've been able to take that aptitude and lessons learned and apply them to new opportunities.

How can you make being committed to excellence a core strength in your day-to-day life? Do you currently have this as a core strength?

____

____

____

____

____

CARING LEADER: KNOWING WHEN TO LEAD AND WHEN TO FOLLOW

He who can't be a good follower cannot be a good leader."

– Aristotle

Taking care of those you are fortunate to lead is a core strength of those in the military. Our people are our number one resource that will make or break a task, mission, or organization. As a leader, getting to know your subordinates personally is very important. You will make better judgment calls based on a particular reaction or an interaction that doesn't reflect an individual's typical behavior.

Ensuring that the employees who work for you have all the resources they need to grow is important. When your employees confront obstacles, it's up to you, as a leader, to remove those barriers to their success. This will increase the trust between you and those you are leading.

There will be times when, as a leader, you have to rely solely on the expertise and advice of those who report to you to meet the mission requirements. This could be for one of several reasons:

- You are new to the organization.
- You don't have the expertise in a particular area.
- You are not going to be available when critical decisions must be made

So being a good follower is just as important as being a good leader. Your direct reports will want to see that you respect their abilities, skills, and knowledge to make decisions. This will allow you as a leader to build depth within your team to ensure that at a moment's notice the same message will be delivered in your absence.

A key skill of a leader is to develop the leaders around you. This requires you to both lead and follow. A great leader will spend a good amount of time building up and supporting the leaders around them, so they have a plan to ensure the mission may be accomplished in their absence.

There are many benefits to knowing when to lead and when to follow:

- Mutual respect is developed.
- Relying on the subject matter experts you surround yourself with brings success.

- Ownership spreads through all level of the organization.
- It shows you trust others' abilities.
- It opens the situation up to the best possible outcome.

For example, as an executive in the information technology field, your technical expertise will diminish over time. While you spend a majority of your time working on strategy and taking care of your staff, technology continues to change – rapidly. You cannot be as technically effective, so you put on your follower's role and trust those you supervise to lead the charge, make critical decisions, and advise you on the proper use of technology in the organization. It is no longer possible in today's environment to stay hands on with the cutting edge of technology *and* be a credible executive creating strategy.

Your role as an executive is to take care of your people and remove obstacles while they put in place the new technology required. You may be challenged as you experience the typical stages of a transition: letting go of old ways, discovering how to be who you need to be, and embracing who you are becoming. You must learn to shift between being a leader and being a follower.

Are you being a good follower and trusting in the expertise of those you surround yourself with? If not, what can you do to ensure you build this core strength?

____

____

____

____

____

INTEGRITY: COMMITMENT TO HUMILITY AND BEING A TEAM PLAYER

"If you don't have integrity, you have nothing. You can't buy it. You can have all the money in the world, but if you are not a moral and ethical person, you really having nothing."

– Henry Kravis

Integrity is a core strength of any military member or veteran. A common definition for integrity is *the quality of being honest and having high moral principles; moral uprightness.* This applies whether you are alone or in a group. In the military, integrity can never be compromised. You must trust that the soldier to your left or your right will be a team player and make the right decisions. This is not always the case for the general population.

We have all been tempted to do things that we know take us out of our commitment to integrity.

In the news every day we hear of a large corporation with an integrity issue at the top; in some cases the leadership forced their employees to take actions that were not in line with their personal values, taking them out of integrity.

In the 2016 presidential race, we saw candidates called out for a lack of integrity or acting out of integrity to meet their own agendas. This is a critical core strength for the leader of the free world that must not be taken lightly.

Acting in integrity also requires the ability to be humble and a good team player – no matter what. Sometimes people make decisions that are out of integrity just because they are not supportive of others' leadership or decisions. They believe they are the one who should be in charge and make the decisions, so they will attempt to do undermining activities, even at the cost of their personal integrity.

There are many benefits to having integrity as core strength:

- You quickly become someone that others can trust and want to follow.
- Great things are entrusted to you.
- You will create valuable interpersonal relationships at all levels of an organization and in your personal life.
- You can feel good about your decisions, no matter what.
- You are seen as a role model for others.

You will be tempted to make decisions and take actions that are not in integrity, such as witnessing something illegal and choosing to not report it to the authorities; turning away from a bad situation because you don't want to get involved, even though you know it will have negative consequences for someone else; not owning up to a wrong decision because it's a hit to your ego, etc. This is where as humans we are put to the test to see what we will do, even if no one is watching. Your true integrity is defined by the choices you make, even when no one else will know.

Where does your integrity lie in tough situations? Are you following "true North" in your veteran's built-in moral compass?

____

____

____

____

____

ABILITY TO INFLUENCE: UNDERSTANDING WHAT OTHERS NEED AND PROVIDING SERVICE AND SUPPORT THAT BENEFITS BOTH SIDES

"Leadership is influence."

– John Maxwell

Influence: what a powerful concept! History has shown that this can have both a negative and positive implication, depending on how it's used. Our nation has played a significant role in shaping how the world operates, particularly as we protect our allies. Our military involvement has strongly influenced our relationships with other countries. The wars in Iraq and Afghanistan have required that our military leadership support the citizens and military forces of those nations to take and maintain control of their future for their own safety and growth. This is a challenging core strength to develop, as there is a fine line between manipulation and influence. Your integrity will guide you to know the difference and support you to do what will best support both sides.

The definition of influence, *the capacity to affect the character, development, or behavior of someone or something, or the effect itself,* focuses on the result. When exercising influence, always keep the result in mind.

This core strength is not only important in the military but also in the corporate world. The ability to influence change, build consensus, or create a dedicated following is important to survival in any industry. You will see cases in the corporate environment where the use of influence results in manipulation or pushing a personal agenda.

There are many benefits to developing influence as a core strength:

- Habits will develop that attract like-minded people.
- You will be seen as a trusted leader.
- You will have a positive effect on those around you.
- You will empower others.

On several occasions, I have been brought into an organization to quickly turn around poorly performing departments or contracts to avoid significant adverse results. My first task is to observe the environment. I want a good feel for the situation without any biases that those involved might bring to my attention. My goal is not to affect the change required, but rather to *influence* those in the situation to affect the change themselves. One technique I've found useful to influence change is to ask a lot of questions. This allows the individuals to discover the problems themselves and identify a change. They become empowered because they have identified the crux of the problem and determined what they need to do to fix it.

In the end, employees must own the change process and be prepared to carry on the required changes when I am no longer involved in the process. At times, I may influence existing leadership to change out those who are not going to be part of the solution.

Where have you had a positive influence on the outcome of a situation? Is this a core strength you are looking to enhance? If so, what are some actions you plan to take?

____

____

____

____

____

UNDERSTANDING THE USE OF EMOTIONAL INTELLIGENCE: ABILITY TO EFFECTIVELY MANAGE YOUR EMOTIONS AND INTERPERSONAL RELATIONSHIPS

Emotional intelligence, sometimes called EQ, is a core strength that can serve veterans well during and after transition. This strength is a fundamental way of "being" that most people don't understand or try to develop. Emotional intelligence entails the following four areas:

Self-Awareness - Your ability to accurately perceive your emotions and stay aware of them as they happen. This includes how you tend to respond to specific situations and certain people.

Self-Management - Your ability to use awareness of your emotions to stay flexible and positively direct your behavior. This means managing your emotional reactions to all situations and people.

Social Awareness - Your ability to accurately pick up on emotions in other people and perceive what is really going on. This often means understanding what other people are thinking and feeling, even if you don't feel the same way.

Relationship Management - Your ability to use awareness of your emotions and the emotions of others to manage interactions successfully. Accurate emotional awareness can guide clear communication and effective handling of conflict.

The first two areas involve your personal competence and the second two involve your social competence. They can positively impact your ability to build important relationships as you transition from the military and set yourself up for success in a new, unfamiliar career.

The benefits of highly developed emotional intelligence as a core strength include:

- The ability to grow and engage your network.
- Flexibility to respond to others to get the best results, rather than reacting.
- Understanding why others may react in unexpected ways.
- The ability to facilitate diverse situations and people under adverse conditions.

Your military service has prepared you with highly developed emotional intelligence to make critical decisions that could essentially make or break an outcome. Your high EQ sets you far ahead of just about anyone else in a corporate environment.

I have used EQ both in the military and my civilian career, and on many occasions, I have had to be on my game in each of the four areas.

I exercised **self-awareness** as a professional, keeping my thoughts and emotions in check no matter what the situation was.

I practiced **self-management**, which included being flexible and looking for a positive win-win outcome for all involved.

Not only did I have to manage my own emotions, but I also had to be aware of how others are managing theirs. (Or not!) Those you work with may not be as skilled at these four areas of emotional intelligence, which requires you to be even better at them. This **social awareness** is critical in times of stress and when making important decisions.

You can leverage this social awareness to build and encourage positive relationships in your professional environment, creating dynamic leadership results. This is **relationship management**.

Take time to document a personal assessment of your EQ in each of these four areas and create an action plan to get closer to where you want to be.

EFFECTIVE COMMUNICATION: BUILD AND SUSTAIN RAPPORT WITH ALL PERSONALITY STYLES AND RANKS

"I'm a great believer that any tool that enhances communication has profound effects in terms of how people can learn from each other, and how they can achieve the kind of freedoms that they are interested in."

– Bill Gates

Communication can be your friend or your foe depending on how well you develop the core strength. There are many types of communication; written, verbal, body language, etc. This is a strength that you will work to hone your entire life; mastering or perfecting is not possible. An infinite number of situations and conditions can come into play at any time during communication. Even tightly scripted speeches can go off track if you slip and use the wrong word, if your audience misinterprets what you are trying to say, if you experience an unexpected interruption, if you are bridging culture barriers, etc.

Military personnel and veterans are highly qualified communicators. Constant exposure to situations with unpredictable outcomes trains them to be hyper-sensitive to what they say and do. They also must build and sustain a healthy rapport up and down their chain of command regardless of another's rank, attitude, or behavioral styles.

Have you seen someone talk to their superiors one way, their peers another way, and their direct reports yet another way? Perhaps this person speaks with deference to a superior, in a casual tone to peers, and with a tone of superiority to an employee. You can imagine the confusion this can create in a work environment.

There should be no difference in your communication abilities and style based on the position of who you are interacting with. People you interact with like to know that, regardless of their position on an organizational chart or their age, they will be treated with respect and dignity when communicating with you.

There are many benefits to being a great communicator:

- The ability to communicate up, down, and across brings everyone together.
- Flattening the "structure" builds sustainable, positive relationships.
- Effective communication brings to life the one-team concept.
- It breaks down barriers that prohibit effectiveness.

As my career in information technology progressed, it became evident that at each step I needed to change and evolve my communication skills. Starting out, I was able to write and speak the tech language as well as anyone. As I began managing people, I had to learn how to communicate my vision, approach, expectations, etc., if I expected anyone to follow me. Next, I had to learn to speak effectively to the business and political priorities of those senior to me in the organization. This was fundamentally important, but my personal style and my technical background made it a challenge. I quickly realized that if I did not succeed in making this change, it would ultimately have a negative impact on my career. In time, this became one of my greatest strengths. Now I can look back and see that each year I continue to improve my communication abilities.

How would you currently rate your communication level and style? Do you see areas that may be holding you back? How can you focus on them and improve?

____

____

____

____

____

DISPLAYING ADAPTABILITY: BE OPEN AND RESPECTFUL OF OTHER PEOPLE'S IDEAS AND CAPABILITIES

"Adaptability is being able to adjust to any situation at any given time."

– John Wooden

As I was starting out in the military, very early in my adult life, I struggled when things rarely came out the way I intended or hoped for. I had developed a very fixed mindset as a youth. I couldn't see more than one way (my way!) to do a task. I would get frustrated when others would do the same task differently. Even if they got the same result (or even a better one), it didn't sit well with me. Others often would perceive my frustration as disrespect for their ideas and capabilities, resulting in bad personal and professional relationships.

The military taught me adaptability. As a service member, you are put into situations for which you may have no control, be it the process, the outcome, or the environment. I had two choices: develop the ability to be adaptable or live a very painful existence amongst those that could.

I developed a practice of coming up with three plans: Plan A, Plan B, and Plan C. This gave me some internal flexibility, making it easier to not get set on a particular outcome. I came to realize that often my plan A was not the best plan. Not being tied to a particular outcome became much more satisfying. This alleviated a lot of stress and angst over trying to force a particular outcome.

There are many benefits to displaying adaptability:

- You attract like-minded people that are similarly adaptable.
- Things that you haven't thought of will be exposed.
- You gain flexibility to adapt to others solutions.
- Communication lines will remain open.
- Mutual respect will be established and flourish.

Veterans have been exposed to this core skill and can bring adaptability to bear in most situations. This makes them great employees and leaders who can be open to respecting and accepting others' ways of achieving results and, ultimately, success.

What are your weaknesses in being adaptable? Do you become too attached to particular outcomes?

____

____

____

____

____

SUCCESS IN STRESSFUL SITUATIONS: KNOWING THAT YOU HAVE ENDURED AND SUCCEEDED IN SIMILAR HIGH-STRESS SITUATIONS

"Just because we are in a stressful situation doesn't mean that we have to get stressed out. You may be in a storm. The key is, don't let the storm get in you."

– Joel Osteen

Most people have no shortage of stressful situations. Turn on the news, read any social media platform, talk to people, or just get in your car – stressful situations will make themselves known. While in the military, you experience extreme conditions that an average citizen will only see on television. The military teaches you how to handle yourself in high-stress situations and take care of those in your charge.

Stress can be seen as the confusion created when the mind overrides the body's basic desires. Your mindset is critical to how you deal with situations; you must look for a positive mindset.

Few professions will put you in a life-and-death situation and expect you to perform as flawlessly as possible. You can take this experience into a civilian career and provide a new perspective on how to appropriately deal with stress.

There are many benefits to the core strength of managing stress:

- Your health will remain a priority.
- You will be able to lead others through the tough situations.
- The ultimate solution will be found – not lost in chaos.
- You have experiences that will prove very valuable as you influence the future.

I want to share one personal example that shows how you can turn your most stressful situation into a huge positive for your future. After 9/11, I was part of two Combatting Terrorism teams for different federal agencies fighting the newest form of war at the time. I was a federal contractor responsible for setting up and managing the information technology infrastructure to provide real-time intelligence to those deployed around the world in combat missions.

This 24x7 high-availability environment required everyone involved to operate in the most stressful of situations one hundred percent of the time. This required me to adapt and grow quickly in all of my skill sets. It was imperative that I be at my very best to support the war fighter who was boots on the ground in the theater.

I grew physically and mentally exhausted, on the verge of passing out at times, because of the high stress level and long hours. But the mission was too important to succumb to the negative effects. I had to better manage myself to stay in the fight for the long haul. In the end being able to operate effectively under stress has provided great advantages to being able to work very unique programs and thrive in the process.

This experience has shaped every aspect of my life since and will continue to for the rest of my life. I have been in several high-stress situations since, and I have been even more successful because I leveraged my past experiences. Without these high-stress experiences, I would not have the ability to put other experiences into perspective.

What is your current level of stress? Are you properly managing the negative effects of stress in your life? What can you do to improve how you are handling stress? Do you have prior experiences you can leverage for future situations?

____

____

____

____

____

EMBRACE LIFELONG LEARNING: QUICKLY GRASPING NEW TECHNICAL AND LEADERSHIP KNOWLEDGE

"The capacity to learn is a gift; the ability to learn is a skill; the willingness to learn is a choice."

– Brian Herbert

Growing up, many of us don't exactly enjoy going to school and learning. Why is that? I couldn't stand going to school and learning. I had horrible grades in elementary school and just better-than-horrible grades in middle school. Until I found out why – and the answer is different for everyone – I was unable to be successful. Structured learning, as it was designed and pushed on the students, was not working for me. I had to learn how to learn my way, not the way a group of people decided was the "right way," based solely on their experience and some study (that was performed more than likely before I was born).

Once I figured that out, I was well on my way to great success in lifelong learning. My passion grew stronger with each degree and certification I completed. These were propelling me along at a good speed in an industry that was very competitive: information technology. By the time I finished my master's degree, I had a 4.0 GPA and was accepted into a Ph.D. program. I now read at least two to three books a month – a mix of self-development, business, and pleasure.

When we get on our desired career path, we need to continue to learn and grasp new concepts more quickly than ever before. If we let ourselves become stagnant in knowledge, our career growth will stagnate, too.

Military veterans have been exposed to situations that require them to continue to learn, grow, and adapt at a moment's notice. They can take this core skill with them into any situation and be a huge standout success. As service members transition to the civilian sector, they face many situations that require them to learn new concepts and skill sets. This is a daunting task, but with the various other core strengths a veteran possesses, this is achievable.

There are many benefits to having the core skill of lifelong learning:

- You step in front of those who are not learning new concepts.
- You stay abreast of changes and more easily adapt to them.

- You have a leg up in interviews and consideration for internal promotions.
- Your brain flourishes because of its neuroplasticity

Extensive studies on the neuroplasticity of the human brain have proven that the brain is not static and shaped only at a particular point in development. The brain has the capacity to grow over time with constant learning and exercising of its functionality.

As a veteran, you can put these study results to the test and make lifelong learning a core strength that will propel you into a successful future as well.

How do you practice lifelong learning in your daily life? What can you be doing to improve in this area?

____

____

____

____

____

BEING AN IMMEDIATE CONTRIBUTOR – PROACTIVELY POSITIONING YOURSELF TO BE READY WHEN NEEDED

"We all need to feel that we are contributing value to the lives of others."

– Dan Brule

When a service member arrives at a new duty station, they find themselves thrown among others who have been there for any amount of time. To be productive and provide as much value as possible at your new assignment, learn to quickly come up to speed in many ways: understand your role, understand your structure, get a feel for any dependencies, understand the overall vision and how that fits your approach, become familiar with the hottest topics, etc. You have a lot of information to process in a short period – on top of moving and settling into your new living quarters to ensure your family has the chance to adjust and get their needs taken care.

This, over time, becomes a core strength of all service members, and they can do most of it without thinking. They can mentally plan and anticipate most situations after a couple of duty station changes, especially those who have been deployed to support a mission overseas. You are hypersensitive to becoming an immediate contributor to the mission and serving those around you.

There are many benefits to being an immediate contributor:

- Anticipating where an organization is going puts you in the driver's seat.
- Your value as an employee increases exponentially.
- The projects and people entrusted to you will flourish.
- Leadership will come to rely on this quality.

As we all know, in the corporate sector it's all about results. To be ready to take on an organization's latest challenges, you need to learn how you can provide an immediate contribution. Then you need to be able to step back and do it again because change and forward movement are non-stop. The question is, *What have you done for me lately?* You will have an answer because you bring the core skill of being an immediate contributor to your job.

I worked in the information technology field for more than twenty years. The IT field demands the ability to learn and contribute to the latest and greatest technology evolutions. If an organization's technology lags behind, the business will suffer. It is critical that the IT department stays on the forefront, contributing proactively to the future of the organization, or it will lose its competitive edge. The demand for immediate contributors never stops. I've gone into organizations or managed contracts with the intent of making an immediate contribution to pull the organization out of its evolutionary stagnation and move it forward.

Are you honing the core skill of being an immediate contributor? If so, you will be noticed for being able to solve critical problems and add significant value to your organization.

Would you be considered an immediate contributor? If not, where do you feel you need to improve?

____

____

____

____

____

Key Takeaways

1. Core strengths are critical elements of who you are as a veteran.
2. Each of these core strengths will provide many benefits to your success.
3. You can use these core strengths to describe the value you will bring to any organization.
4. Be less concerned and focused on matching technical skills or corporate know-how and more focused on the soft skills.
5. These core strengths are representative of those of a proven leader; use them to your advantage.
6. Don't hesitate to identify other core strengths you have developed that may be just as important to your future success.
7. You will run into those that do not share these core strengths; be a role model by continuing to model them.
8. Focus on your strengths versus trying to overcome your weaknesses.
9. Know that you bring a set of strengths that are vital to the success of any organization.
10. Organizations that include hiring and supporting veterans as a strategic objective will identify with the strengths you have developed in the military.

Part II

AIM – Plan Your Transition and Prepare for Your Future

CREATE A LONG-TERM PLAN VERSUS A QUICK FIX

A successful transition requires that you be focused on the long term so you can discover the best options for you and your family. When you entered military service, you may not have known exactly what was ahead of you, but you knew you were vested in a successful outcome for the long term, whether it was two years or twenty. Transitioning to a civilian career may take some time as you discover your ideal path. Everyone's transition is different, with varying levels of complexity. You need to do what will serve you best in the long term.

You may be tempted to choose a job that is a quick fix, not one that aligns with your values or vision. But quick fixes typically are not sustainable, and they will not serve you over time. Competing requirements may push you to make short-term decisions to pay the bills, find a temporary place to live, adjust to different environments, handle medical or disability challenges, etc. Don't let these short-term demands pull you away from your ideal plan and strategy.

Your long-term plan should be seen as your personal vision, and this should be tightly aligned with your values. Take the time to see and hear your values reflected as you develop your long-term plan. Be sure to write down your plan so you can refer back to it as you are progressing. Your long-term plan will be a living document that changes over time as your circumstances change and as the clarity of what is in front of you becomes sharper. There will be many holes to fill in along the way, and it will seem incomplete in the sense that you don't have all the answers up front. That is the great thing about creating a long-term plan: you can allow yourself to evolve without tying yourself into something that may not be what you want

As all military veterans know, tactical and strategic plans are keys to success. Equally important are a guide for the short-term completion of tactical items and a vision for the long-term strategy. You want to align yourself with key resources that will support the various areas of your plan so you can be efficient, not reinvent the wheel, or go down a path that doesn't take you where you want to go. It's never too late to create a plan and put key actions into play.

These steps will help you create your transition plan:

- Take time to reflect on where you have been and where you want to go.
- Understand who you need to be to reach your vision, and list your values and strengths.
- Create a bold future- and value-based vision statement that stretches you.

- Create a list of five goals that will help you achieve your vision over time. Make these goals large enough to be measurable but keep them attainable.
- Align yourself with people who can help you be successful in reaching your vision.
- GO.... Get started.... Make it happen!!

CREATE STRUCTURE

What is the single most prominent element you are exposed to when you enter into the military? Structure. It's not something that comes naturally or is part of most people's lives. As you move through basic training, specialty training, and into various duty assignments, you realize how important it is to have structure. No matter your background, you come to rely on the benefits of a structure. Because the military requires accountability that may not necessarily be part of civilian life, structure becomes essential. As you look to transition from the military, the apparent lack of structure in the civilian world can be daunting. You may be able to exist and even thrive without much structure, but it certainly is a valuable tool for success. Without structure, you can take on too many tasks and responsibilities, leading to an unsatisfying life. So how do you create a structure that works for you as an individual when you are used to having a structure that was based on a team approach?

Your personal structure for success should have the same aspects of the organizational structure you operate within for the military:

Plan. Set the goals that support your vision. This will be your operating framework. Your plan should be a living document you can adjust at any time. Without one, you will have no direction.

Processes and Procedures. Create consistent processes and procedures for getting things done in your life, whether it's personal or professional. Scheduling these processes and procedures will indicate how long it will take to accomplish particular tasks and give you confidence that you can achieve them.

People. Surround yourself with those who will consistently support you and urge you on to the next level. These should be people who will push you to be your best but are also willing to pick you up when you stumble, fall, or outright fail.

Accountability. Find ways to make sure you and the people you surround yourself with can hold you accountable to stay on track and be successful. You don't want to get so far off track that you feel lost or that you are not achieving what you planned.

You will have your preferred level of structure. For some, the more structure they can build into their life the better they are. Others only require a basic amount of structure to stay focused and confident. You may find that you can fluctuate your level of structure, depending on what is going on, to ensure your success. Don't feel there is a "right answer" when it comes to the type or amount of structure. Allow yourself the ability to determine what is right for you regardless of what others are doing or thinking.

CREATE A SUPPORT NETWORK

The military does a great job providing an integrated support network for all the resources you need, whether it is fellow soldiers supporting each other, groups for spouses, deployment support groups, groups that provide dependents support, etc. This becomes a way of life for those in the military, and you become accustomed to this level of support. These types of groups exist outside the military, but they don't carry the same level of camaraderie and understanding that exists in the military support networks. This can become an eye-opening experience for those who have been in for some time or have been deployed for numerous deployments.

When transitioning out of the military, it is vital to describe in writing the support network you currently have that is making you successful. As part of this process, identify where you believe you could use stronger support to bolster those areas that are more challenging for you.

Some of the areas to consider for establishing post-transition support networks include, but are not limited to:

- Other transitioning veterans
- Family and friends
- Career field-based
- Mentors and coaches
- Medical, dental, legal, financial
- Hobby-related
- Social media groups

For each of your groups, identify a minimum of one to two people that you know you can lean on for support. Be sure to reach out to them and have a conversation about where you are in your transition and how you believe they could be of great help in this process. Most people are honored to provide whatever support they can for someone they know has served our great country and is now transitioning to a new future. Over time, be sure to work on expanding the areas and people within your support network. Keep in mind that quality over quantity will serve you best. Don't add a lot of people who could "potentially" support you. Only ask those who agree to actively support you to be part of your network.

Many benefits can come from having an established support network before fully transitioning from the military:

- Reduced or eliminated stress/anxiety
- Peace of mind knowing you have someone to turn to
- A greater sense of being part of a new community
- Potential referrals for jobs

Remember to be transparent about your needs with your support network and provide support to them where you can. Be sure to keep an open mind on how things will go in various situations and know that things will be different, but that's ok.

CREATE A SOCIAL LIFE

The camaraderie and connection to those you serve with are like nothing you will ever experience, especially in an organized corporate cultural setting. A robust social life is a key to fulfillment. The military provides places to gather socially, teams for sports, groups for families, etc. These can also be found in the civilian sector, but you need to be more conscious of the selection, as they are not necessarily as structured or connected by a similar belief or value system.

Today you hear the familiar term *tribe* to describe people who have something in common and share a value system. It's like a pack from an animal's perspective. Some tribes and packs are more open to those that are not exactly like them in every way, while others are very tight, only letting in those they feel meet their values, or in the case of animals, their species.

The military is excellent at providing various social opportunities within the base or organization to which you are assigned. By being assigned to that base or organization, you are accepted as a member but still expected to conform to the culture. When you get out into civilian life, there are many cultures and subcultures to join. Again, some are very open while others may include only those who share a certain belief structure or set of criteria. Knowing what social groups exist within these cultures and subcultures can be quite challenging.

As you become acclimated to a new way of living, a social life is essential. This serves you in many ways:

- A place to feel part of a greater cause
- A way to contribute to the community you have become a part of
- Not feeling alone
- In some ways, continuing the camaraderie you have enjoyed

There are a few things to keep in mind when you decide what kind of social life to develop or be part of:

- Ensure that it adheres to your values and morals so that you can be proud of what you socially take part in.
- Don't restrict yourself to only what you know and are used to; be open to new or different ways.
- Understand that within the new social life you form, there will be differences in backgrounds and opinions.
- Only look to develop a social life that fits your nature. Bigger and bolder is not always best for those who prefer smaller circles of interaction.

You don't always have to "find" a group to belong to! Be the leader you have been trained to be and start a social group. Lead the way to develop something that other veterans will be drawn to, and that may even have a national presence.

CREATE A FINANCIAL WELLNESS PLAN

When transitioning from the military, it's important to understand all aspects of your finances to ensure that you can provide for your family and meet all the financial obligations you may be carrying over with you. There is a difference between what you take home in the military and what you will take home in the civilian sector. In the military, there are portions of your income that are not taxed, while in the civilian sector most of your income is taxed. This can be a big shock to veterans who don't realize or understand how significant the tax break is from housing and food allowances.

There are some steps you should take when building your financial plan:

Step 1 – If you have not already done so, document all the expenses you incur on a monthly, quarterly, and annual basis. Include in these expenses your daily living costs for food, transportation, entertainment, etc.

Step 2 – Determine your savings goals for cash on hand, retirement, and education (if applicable).

These are just as important as any debt you know you have to pay.

Step 3 – Determine the geographical location where you intend to live. Learn the average cost for a house or rental, based on your needs; the average salary in that area for the industry you plan to work in, and any other locality-based costs that may be relevant.

Step 4 – Once you have collected this information – debt, savings goals, and anticipated income – put them together in a cohesive monthly budget and see how the actual numbers compare to your expectations.

Step 5 – Make any adjustments necessary to bring your financial plan in line with the income you realistically anticipate earning. You may need to contact a financial advisor or use an online financial tool to determine estimates on federal, state, and local tax brackets and average premiums for the various benefits you may receive.

Step 6 – Set some milestones to adjust your living to this financial plan. Execute with passion, as this is your future!

Your financial goals should be both near-term and long-term. Having goals and actions that will set you up for financial independence is key to living a fulfilling life. Don't develop a plan based on keeping up with the Joneses or having all those things you always wished you could afford. In time, and with the right planning and execution, this will all be possible. I would highly encourage you to estimate costs and income conservatively, so your plan is executable.

CREATE AN EDUCATIONAL WELLNESS PLAN

We've all heard the saying "knowledge is power." This is especially true in today's world. It is important to continue your education and earn the requisite certifications and degrees for the field you choose to work in. Ongoing education proves your level of knowledge and your commitment to growing and becoming your best. As someone who frequently reviews resumes, I look to see what types of education and certifications the candidate has pursued and achieved.

One of the most significant benefits the military provides is the GI Bill. Getting your education paid for is rare – and a smart thing to pursue. During my years of service, I saw many active duty members not taking advantage of this amazing benefit. Because deployments, shift work, and variable schedules can make it difficult to pursue a degree, you have the option to use it once you separate from the military. Take advantage of it!

While you certainly can gain a professional position as a result of knowledge, more importantly, it positions you to be in charge of your future. You will be less reliant on others to inform you of what they believe may be best for you. You will gain an intense amount of inner confidence and peace of mind as you continue to learn. Learning something new every day is a powerful way of life.

As adults, we need to be continually learning from those who have taken the time to document what they know. Not only will you benefit from your increasing level of knowledge, but you will be able to help anyone who comes in contact with you. People will look to you as an expert in an area, and this will help propel you to levels you never thought would exist in your future. There are many proven health benefits to exercising your mental abilities as well.

"In your thirst for knowledge, be sure not to drown in all the information."

– Anthony D'Angelo

When I was young, I planned to just get a job, specifically in the military, and I assumed that would give me all I needed to live a comfortable life. Fortunately for me, I was able to see my error in judgment. Shortly after entering the military, I started on my first degree, which ultimately led to three degrees and being accepted into a Ph.D. program (along with a laundry list of certifications).

Instead of allowing my past failures to define my future successes, I decided to figure out why I did so poorly in my early school years. Many reasons led to disappointing outcomes, but one of my challenges was learning how to learn. While that may sound like an odd statement, there is a lot of value in it. I didn't know how to take the information as it was presented and figure out how I could learn and apply it. Once I learned how to do that, I went from Cs and Ds in elementary school to a 4.0 GPA on my master's degree. Had I allowed my past to influence my future, I would not have made the investments I did in education.

Countless veterans who have successfully transitioned have told me that you must shore up your education and do this proactively so that you are positioned for the best opportunities possible.

Key Takeaways

1. Plan, plan, plan. And plan some more.
2. Start early in your preparations for separation.
3. Know you will encounter obstacles, but you are prepared to deal with them.
4. Start building your veteran-based network and grow it as you progress.
5. Do not isolate yourself during the transition process. Many organizations and individuals are willing to partner for your success.
6. Think long term.
7. Ensure you include your loved ones' needs and desires as part of your comprehensive plan.
8. Don't be hooked on one single outcome; be open to options or alternatives solutions.
9. Keep pushing when things seem disconnected or lack direction.
10. Understand that you are going through three very common phases when you are in transition: leaving behind a successful career, determining and executing your future, and starting your new career.

Part III

FIRE! It's Go Time. Execute the Investment in You

It's time to invest in you!

Life goes by too quickly to be idle on the sidelines saying: "I will get to that as soon as...," "I really want to be able to...," or "Once I get through... I will get this started." You always will have countless reasons to postpone investing in and taking care of yourself. Of course, when someone else asks for support in getting started on an investment they are making in themselves, no doubt you are ready, willing, and make the time. You need to assign this same sense of urgency and importance to yourself.

If someone were to ask you, "How much are you worth?" or "What is your value?" do you have an answer? Or would you stand there with thoughts racing and self-limiting beliefs in the lead? You must place a value on your time and yourself as a being. As with any investment you care about, you want that value to increase over time and become something you are proud of. As you know, this will not just happen on its own. A personal investment requires a significant amount of dedication and commitment to achieve.

"When you learn how much you are worth, you will stop giving people discounts."

– Preston Smiles

Investing in you is of no less value than investing in stocks and bonds! Even the smallest of returns shows there is value to be recognized. Two common excuses people use when they don't invest in themselves are no time no money. Make sure as you plan your schedule and budget you have both time and money set aside to strategically and smartly invest in yourself for your future.

I define investing as *providing or endowing yourself with a particular skill or attribute*. These skills and attributes will keep you going when your path gets steep and rocky – and it will. You will need to be diligent in championing your personal growth and future.

This doesn't mean that you should forsake others in any way, as that's contrary to growing yourself. I've had many clients who feel that if they take an ounce of time for themselves or put a serious and intentional focus on themselves, they are selfish. Consequently, they neglect their growth, and that leads to dissatisfaction. Your intentions should always be transparent; choose to move *toward* a compelling goal, rather than *avoiding* a less desirable outcome or consequence. Ensure that your approach is all about what *you* are doing and release any of the "could do, will do, should do" mindset that will hold you back.

Diligence + Focused Efforts = Success

There are many ways in which you can invest in yourself. These are the ones I recommend. They will grow you personally and professionally and will be deeply rewarding:

- Enhance your relationship with money
- Create an insatiable thirst for knowledge
- Improve your focus on leisure and recreation
- Dress for success
- Expand your connectedness
- Eliminate internal and external distractions
- Improve your overall health
- Recharge your inner strength

To paint a clear picture of what each of these areas could encompass, I will share a personal example for each one. There are many ways to achieve the same goal, so don't be tied to my examples as the only ways. I provide these to inspire you, motivate you, provide a basis for understanding, and spark some ideas that you can apply to your situation. An exercise follows each idea to get you started in the areas you feel need attention.

ENHANCE YOUR RELATIONSHIP WITH MONEY

You have probably heard that money talks.... Well, it sure does when you don't seem to have enough or are not handling what you have properly. Your relationship with money can make or break your future. You must learn how to make money grow and build passive income. Investing your money wisely puts it to work for you. While your investments increase and build passive income, you can put your attention on actively positioning yourself for success in other ways without being distracted by handling the money you already have. It's a discipline that can pay enormous dividends in the future – to support your family, go to college, buy a house, buy a car, or prepare for retirement.

For many, it is challenging to find the right balance, and for many reasons. There are many demands for the money you make, and the uncertain economy has not allowed employers to give significant raises.

When I was starting out, I chased happiness through spending; of course, that never truly brought me lasting happiness. All too often, within days of making a significant purchase, I would find myself with buyer's remorse, wishing I had saved the money. My Achilles heel on spending money for happiness was to buy new vehicles. Between the money down and the cost of making a change in insurance, add-ons to the vehicle, etc., I would spend way more than I had anticipated. I frequently relied on credit for emergency situations. And I was almost always unsatisfied with my choices.

"Your financial situation is a reflection of your HIDDEN relationship with money."

– Morgana Rae

As I grew older, this became a bigger issue, and I decided I needed to significantly improve my relationship with my money. As soon as I transitioned from the military in my mid-twenties, I established a 401(k) retirement account to ensure that someday I will be able to retire and comfortably enjoy my later years. Each year I made the maximum contribution, even if it meant I had to delay a purchase and be more conservative on my spending. It was a challenge to fight the urge to spend on something I really didn't need, buy something I wanted, or take an expensive vacation. Depositing the money into an account that was not accessible made it much easier.

While many people bailed on the stock market during the recession, I did the opposite and kept my foot on the gas. Now, as the economy slowly recovers from one of the worst downturns in history, my current balances show that this was a smart idea.

Holding a long-term focus as I have invested my money has proven to be a true blessing to achieving financial security. My internal compelling vision is to know that when I retire, I did all I could to prepare for this time while I was working.

What will you have to adjust to put enough money into savings?

If you've never drawn up a budget, here is a great way to get started. List all your monthly expenses in the left column. On the right, identify each one as living, recreational, or investing.

Expense (Amount)	**Type (Living, Recreational, Investing)**

Once you have identified and categorized your expenses, determine where you may need to make adjustments to get your savings to a comfortable level that will work toward a happy future for you and your family. Over time, review the list of expenses and see if there are some that can be removed entirely or can be reduced even more to increase your savings.

Identify a number that you would ideally like to have in savings. Then take a moment to reflect on this question: If you had $__________ in savings, how would that make you feel?

____

____

____

____

____

CREATE AN INSATIABLE THIRST FOR KNOWLEDGE

I'm sure you have heard it said that knowledge is power. Well, you certainly can gain a professional position as a result of knowledge, but more importantly, it positions you to be in charge of your future. You will be less reliant on others to tell you what they believe is best for you. With that said, you should always seek the counsel of others to ensure you are considering all possible information and scenarios. You will gain an intense amount of inner confidence and peace of mind as you continue to learn. Learning something new every day is not just a saying; it's a powerful way of life. Not only will you benefit from your increasing level of knowledge, but you will be able to help others. People will look to you as an expert in your area, and this will help propel you to levels you never thought would exist in your future. There are many proven health benefits to exercising your mental abilities as well.

"In your thirst for knowledge, be sure not to drown in all the information."

– Anthony D'Angelo

I struggled academically in elementary, middle school, and some in high school, which led me to declare I would *never* go to college. No matter how much I tried, my efforts never seemed to be enough to get into the programs or groups that I wanted to join. I didn't believe in myself, and I didn't have the support I needed to get past my limitations. This took a toll on me over time, and I developed a negative attitude toward continuing education. My plan was just to get a job, specifically in the military, and that would give me all I needed to live a comfortable life.

As I progressed in my career I realized the importance not only of formal education but the simple practice of always reading new material. I began the journey of self-development where I began to read no less than three of the best books possible that were relevant to areas I was personally working to improve. This has become a very sustainable habit and one that I have grown to enjoy. Over time when you have read enough books in the self-development discipline you start to map together overlapping themes. An important aspect that is often overlooked is not only reading the books but putting into practice what is being learned. You can gain an intense amount of information but if you do not practice practical application you are not getting the whole positive experience from the power habit of being a lifelong learner. If you had an unlimited budget and all the time you needed, what would you want to learn?

____

____

____

Are you allowing your past limitations to be an obstacle to your future?

Take the time to create a list of limitations (fears, what-if's, doubts, etc.) you believe are preventing you from expanding your education. Next, identify whether these are actual or self-created.

Limitations	**Real or Self-Created**

For those that are self-created, what can you do to eliminate them and take the first step toward a brighter future by obtaining or expanding your education?

____

____

____

IMPROVE YOUR FOCUS ON LEISURE AND RECREATION

Taking time off not only recharges your internal batteries but also inspires your soul. Experiencing areas and events that are not part of your normal routine can have such huge benefits on opening your mind and creating an excitement to relieve stress. When we get stuck in a daily routine, we tend to shut down our creative juices and become complacent in what we are willing to do. The more willing you are to step out and take interesting trips and experience new things, the more inspired you will be to produce results that will push you forward in your personal and professional life.

I've heard someone say they work between vacations, not take vacations between work. This is a very positive approach, reflecting a belief that work is just a part of what you do rather than all of who you are – unless of course, you are one of the fortunate ones who do what they enjoy for a living.

"The real problem of leisure time is how to keep others from using yours."

– Arthur Lacey

For many years I chose not to take a vacation. I felt that I needed to keep my head down, moving forward and growing my career. We all know the saying "time is money." I became increasingly jaded over time and didn't know why. I just wasn't feeling the pleasure I thought I should with all the hard work and dedication I was showing in my job.

I decided I would venture out on a simple vacation. After the relaxation, downtime, and new life experiences of a true vacation, I came back to work full of energy, new ideas, and a better attitude. Vacations don't have to be expensive or big. Some of the simplest vacations have been just as reenergizing as the bigger ones I have taken. Do what feels right and provides the best return, based on how you feel at the end of the vacation.

Each year I have made it a point to do something I've never done before, even if it's when I return to some of the same vacation spots. The new experiences are what push me to be more open-minded and enjoy the results.

If you could go anywhere in the world and do exactly what you wanted, what would that be?

____

____

____

What limiting beliefs are you struggling with? For example, No one can do what I do?, I can't afford to do anything fun?, I don't know where to go?, I feel guilty because...., etc.

Remember, limiting beliefs are self-imposed. We start to think in a certain way, based on our experiences and the effects of the world around us (events in the news, TV sensationalizing what is right/wrong, friends'/family comments, etc.). Make a list of limiting beliefs and determine what effects they are having on your life.

Limiting Beliefs	**Impact on Life**

Choose one or two that are having the biggest negative impact and determine what you are going to do to remove them from your life.

____

____

____

____

____

DRESS FOR SUCCESS

Do you know how good it feels when you put on clothes that fit just right and look great? You feel great about yourself. This, as part of your daily routine, can give you an edge up with your confidence and how you carry yourself. You don't need to wear expensive clothes. Just pick those things that bring out your best and give you that aura of confidence. People will notice the pep in your step and be more attracted to supporting your needs and efforts.

As much as I loved being in the military, I missed having my own identity reflected in what I wore. I've always gained confidence and felt good when I wore clothes that made me feel successful. Having a wardrobe you are comfortable in, that represents your personality and showcases your confidence, is an integral part of establishing yourself.

I bet you have items you bought that did not fit or look the way you hoped, so you don't feel great wearing them. However, because you spent the money, you feel obligated to wear them, right? This reduces confidence and can even be detrimental if you wear less-than-perfect clothes to an important event.

Investing in apparel that makes you feel confident and prepared doesn't have to be expensive. I often shop at outlets and get my clothes on sale.

This is called "dressing for success." People notice and will comment on how well you are dressed and how you take care of yourself, influencing a positive perception about you overall.

If making a change to your wardrobe was not a financial constraint, what would you do?

Take the time to make an inventory of your success wardrobe, including those items you buy with the intent that they will make you feel confident when you wear them. From that list of items, rank them on a scale of 1 to 5 (1 being "doesn't work" to 5 being "makes me feel confident") to show how they positively affect your confidence when you wear them.

Success Clothes	Ranking (1 to 5)

If you don't have anything in your closet that helps to increase your confidence when you wear it, or your items are averaging less than a 3, take the time to identify what you believe would be the perfect wardrobe and write it down.

____

____

____

____

____

Now work toward this in an economical and thrifty way, one piece at a time.

EXPAND YOUR CONNECTEDNESS

Isolation brings success to no one! But being everyone's "friend" for the sake of having a large network doesn't allow you to be your genuine self. Building a network that is appropriately sized to allow you to be your best will bring many people into your life with common goals and aspirations. Surround yourself with those you have something in common with and who are willing to help you get to the next level. Your network of connections will lead to opportunities that you hadn't seen before.

I've experienced a single connection that led to three relationships and large opportunities and friendships. Without that initial connection, I never would have had those opportunities and friendships. You want to be connected to people at various levels of success. This will allow you to help those who haven't achieved as much success and be helped by those who have achieved more success. You need to focus on surrounding yourself with those that are at the level you are aspiring to grow to will be key to your success. They will provide the value you are seeking in your personal growth. Keep in mind you are where others are aspiring to be and will be looking to gain value from you as well so they can grow.

Valuable relationships will have a profound impact on the quality of your whole life. There is no way to achieve this level of impact without having some level of connectedness.

"If you want to go fast, go alone. If you want to go far, go with others."

– African Proverb

I am an introvert. Building a large network and maintaining numerous relationships has never been my strong suit. For years, I avoided it because I felt uncomfortable in the social situations that were required. Because I could not see the many positive returns I might get from the investment of effort and energy required – and it *is* an effort for an introvert – I would become disengaged.

But when it comes to being connected, it's the quality of those circles that counts, not the quantity.

I changed my approach to suit my nature and focused on growing quality relationships and networks. These smaller circles have provided me an amazing sense of accomplishment, camaraderie, and value. I have increased the size of my circles when I feel comfortable and when it makes sense to my life circumstances. Developing beneficial relationships has been instrumental in making this valuable investment grow. This has opened up professional and personal opportunities that have contributed directly to my overall growth.

Are you engaging with those who can grow your value?

Take some time now to identify those people with whom you are in contact the most and what the relationship is to you.

Individual	**Relationship**

From the list you created above, evaluate each relationship to see what kind of impact this relationship is having on your life. If the effect is not positive, I challenge you to see what can be done to improve the relationship or change its role in your life.

Take the time to identify any relationship gaps you may be experiencing. Relationship gaps may be things such as; nobody at the level you are aspiring to, friends or family that truly support the trajectory you are on; quality support from those around you, etc.

Make a goal to take action on to fill the gap.

____

____

____

____

ELIMINATE INTERNAL AND EXTERNAL DISTRACTIONS

Distractions – both internal and external – can keep you from maintaining the right level of focus and achieving your goals at the rate you desire.

Handling environmental distractions will position you for achieving or exceeding expectations. For example, your physical environment has a surprising impact on your state of mind. One of your greatest distractions may be clutter. Sure, you know you'll get around to organizing your stuff one day, but living in a chaotic environment spills into your daily activities.

An environment that contains distractions limits your success. I've seen people stay in environments they know are not a positive influence or are not providing the needed resources, only to wonder why they are not progressing. For example, stacks of paper and unused items piled around your desk create a sense of incomplete actions or too much to do. Participating in the gossip network at the office turns your mind to negative thoughts versus positive. Allowing someone dictate your career path forward instead of having a collaborative discussion can leave you feeling unfulfilled or disengaged.

Where you live and the quality of your living conditions impacts your well-being. I've lived in many parts of the country and experienced a range of living conditions over the years. I found that when I wasn't living in an environment that represented who I felt myself to be, I was much less happy. As an example, when I moved to the DC area in the military I found the closest apartment. But it wasn't in the best of neighborhoods, and it made me feel out of my element. It had an adverse effect on my life. I'm not sure I understood to what extent this was creating other issues in my life. When I moved to a better maintained and healthier apartment complex, I felt better about being engaged in the community and with the neighbors around me.

"Starve your distractions, feed your focus."

– Unknown

I decided to focus on living in an area in which the homes would appreciate. I also wanted to balance a smart real estate investment with living within my family's means and maintaining sustainable living expenses.

During the crazy housing boom before 2008, my family and I made a deliberate choice to stay in our home, even when houses were selling for double what we had invested. My income had gone up four times since we bought the house. Instead of jumping on the bandwagon and "upgrading" because we could afford it, we took the opposite approach. Once the market started to correct, we refinanced our house and took five years off the existing mortgage at a lower interest rate. This has allowed us to be able to enjoy many opportunities that would not have been possible had we followed the masses that were selling and buying back into the same crazy market.

What would you change about your current environment that would make a consequential impact?

Take the time to reflect on your current living situation. Determine what is not having a positive effect on your life, and then identify an action you can take to change the item.

Areas for Improvement	**Corrective Action**

From this list, pick one or two areas for improvement and make it a point to perform the corrective action you have identified.

IMPROVE YOUR OVERALL HEALTH

You can rarely turn on the TV in the morning and not see an infomercial for an exercise program. They show you before-and-after pictures of what appears to be the same person and ask why everybody isn't following the program they are selling. Typically, the person (if it is the same person!), is in such great shape that it's demotivating for anyone who is more than five "vanity pounds" from what they want to weigh.

Never underestimate the value of investing in your health. Many people believe that exercise and nutrition are just for getting a flat stomach with lots of nice ripples (a six-pack, to be exact). There are so many more benefits, such as stress relief, releasing endorphins that make you feel good, better self-image, better sleep, etc.

A fitness and nutrition program must accommodate your lifestyle so that you do it consistently. Do your best. If that means you do twenty-five reps – or just five – in any given day, then be happy with what your best is. Fitness and nutrition are not areas in which you can compare yourself to anyone, even a relative. Everyone has different daily requirements and a different genetic makeup. The benefits of doing your best to lead a healthy lifestyle are numerous and all positive.

"Exercise is your King and Nutrition is your Queen. Together they create your fitness kingdom."

– Jack LaLanne

It took me years to find an exercise program that works for me. (And I have years of pictures that document the search!) I had smoked for several years, enjoying every bit of it. After I began dating the woman who is now my wife of nineteen years, I quit cold turkey. I have struggled ever since to maintain my ideal weight. I've tried various "diets" and fitness routines, looking for the right combination. None lasted long enough to make a substantial change. While I was switching between various exercise routines, my self-image was poor, and it had negative effects on my life in different ways.

When I was young and much trimmer, I lifted lots of weights, but I didn't get the results I wanted. Next, I tried cardio: exercise bike, running, step machine, treadmill, elliptical, etc. This lasted for a while, but my diet became an issue as I was getting older. So I tried a combination routine: I created a home gym, I was lifting weights and doing cardio on an alternating schedule. This was good but didn't last. Do you recognize the cycle?

One weekend I was watching TV, disgusted with my stress level and exercise routine, when I saw an infomercial on high-intensity interval training. I thought, *Here's the latest craze; how can this be any better?* After seeing it three or four more times, I said, "What the heck," and ordered it. My wife was skeptical, but she decided to try it with me. Three years later, we still do HIIT four to five days a week, and it has become part of our lifestyle. I finally found something that works for me.

I still struggle with my nutrition; I love cookies and chips too much. But the benefits I get from investing in regular exercise and improved (not perfect) diet are beating out my lack of willpower to pass on the cookies and chips.

You can never "out-exercise" bad nutrition. Sticking to a healthy nutritional plan is crucial to achieving maximum results. It's important to find what works for you and make it a part of your lifestyle so that you can enjoy investing in yourself.

How would you feel if you were able to create a lifestyle approach to your health?

Identify several fitness activities that would be engaging and sustainable for your current situation. For each, rate on a scale from 1 to 5 (1 being least satisfying to 5 – this is my new lifestyle) how satisfied you would feel doing this four days a week.

Type of Fitness	Most Satisfying (1 to 5)

Based on the types of activities identified and the ones with the highest appeal, schedule time in your day to work out four days a week.

To improve your nutrition, start by keeping it simple. Look at everything you eat in a given day to determine if it will get you to your goal of better nutrition. See if your portions are reasonable. Use the 80/20 rule to keep yourself on track (80 percent healthy/20 percent indulgence).

RECHARGE YOUR INNER STRENGTH

They say eight hours of sleep a night is the magic number. When was the last time you made it a priority to get enough rest to operate at your best? Is that not where you want to be performing?

Make rest a prime investment in yourself. Resting includes more than sleeping. When you exercise, you rest between runs or sets; then you get up and do it again. Taking your body out of motion and allowing your muscles and mind to go idle is considered rest.

Most of us know we operate at our best with the proper amount of rest, but it's one of the first things we neglect for the benefit of something or someone else. Even slowing down during the day and recharging improves your performance. Going straight out and assuming you will be just fine is not going to benefit you or those you care for. Many people believe that if they are in motion and doing something, they must be ahead of someone and achieving unbelievable results. The opposite is true. Running yourself into the ground can lead to health concerns and even premature death.

I ran myself on the ragged edge for years after I transitioned from military service. A childhood friend commented on how impressed he was with what I had achieved so early in life. Then he said something that got my attention. "At the pace you are going, you will have a heart attack by the time you are thirty." That got my attention! I decided to start considering and implementing tradeoffs that would improve my overall well-being and health.

"Rest and self-care are so important. When you take time to replenish your spirit, it allows you to serve others from the overflow. You cannot serve from an empty vessel."

- Eleanor Brown

I make sure to get no less than seven hours sleep a night. I am very in tune to what my body needs. I allow myself to get more if my body is asking for it through rest intervals during the day. I also ensure that I'm not thinking or physically in motion just because I'm awake, we get so wrapped up in what we are doing and trying to achieve we rarely allow our bodies or minds to go idle. Allowing yourself to mentally and physically recover is very important. I find that without proper levels of rest, I am less effective, handle stress poorly, and can't think as clearly. The results I produce are very poor. I've found a slower and more methodical approach has served me well in reaching the results I desire.

How much more effective could you be if you were getting the rest your body needs?

For each day of the week, write down how many hours of sleep you got and note if you took time to rest during the day. Adjust your habits as necessary to find a balance to feel your best and refreshed throughout the day.

Day of the Week	**Hours of Sleep**	**Rest**

"Investing in yourself is the best investment you will ever make. It will not only improve your life; it will improve lives of all those around you."

– Robin Sharma

I wanted to pose a question and suggest some possible outcomes:

- What is the cost of not investing in you?
- Not achieving the success you desire
- Discontentment with your current situation
- Lack of confidence in yourself and abilities
- Being passed over for promotions
- Failed relationships

- Feelings of isolation
- Making decisions that are not in line with your current situation
- Bouncing between jobs
- Buying and selling cars or houses trying to get that quick fix for feeling better

Can you relate? Eventually, you will become weary of these costs. Recognize that these are missed opportunities. When you invest in your future, these results become less common.

When facing decisions that may be life-altering, we tend to look at the benefit. "If I invest my time and energy, what will I get as a result?"

Asking instead: "What will I miss if I don't?" may be even more enlightening.

Investing in yourself will diminish these costs significantly and ensure maximum returns on your effort. Unlike the stock market, where you have no control over the outcome of your investment, here you can make a profound impact on your own life.

"Invest in as much of yourself as you can; you are your own biggest asset by far."

– Warren Buffett

A genuine inner desire to shift and grow through investing in yourself can:

- Increase your chances for promotion or getting hired into a new field

- Increase your education
- Grow your self-confidence
- Reach your personal and professional goals
- Improve your family's opportunity to achieve desires
- Enhance the lives of those you come in contact with
- Stand out as a role model to others

COMMITMENT + ACHIEVABLE ACTION PLANS = INVESTING IN YOURSELF

Congratulations! If you've hung on and made it this far, enduring my examples, you are probably more committed to starting your self-investment project than just about anyone else. Let's take another look at the areas we've discussed.

- Enhance your relationship with money
- Create an insatiable thirst for knowledge
- Improve your focus on leisure and recreation
- Dress for success
- Expand your connectedness
- Eliminate internal and external distractions
- Improve your overall health
- Recharge your inner strength

Go back through the exercises to assess your current progress and goals.

Which of these areas are part of your life now? Which are you being called to work on? On a scale of 1 to 10, where do you fall in each of these areas?

Does it look more like a mountainous range with some areas being a closer to a 1 and some areas being closer to 10, or have you flat lined with an average of a 5?

Find the time, the money, and the desire to work on and achieve success in at least one area that speaks to your heart. Never try to tackle all areas at once. Being able to focus on and bring a particular area or two up to where you want them for now is more important. If you make investing in yourself part of who you are, this will be an ongoing process. You have been armed with a wealth of knowledge to become an expert marksman in whatever goals you are aiming to achieve. As with any mission you have ever taken on, you must be prepared to take action and move!

"If you put a small value on yourself, rest assured the world will not raise your price."

– Unknown

ACKNOWLEDGEMENTS

I would like to thank my wife, Melisa, and my son, Ty, for all their support and encouragement in creating this resource for veterans. They know how deeply my passion runs, and they continuously cheer me on to success. What I achieve and those I'm able to serve is because of their selfless sacrifice as I give up time with them to do for and be with others.

Melisa and Ty, I appreciate all your love and support – you have given as much to veterans through this work as I. You are true role models for others to follow in what you have done and continue to do as my support structure.

THOUGHT-PROVOKING QUOTES

"Every new beginning comes from some other beginning's end." – Semisonic

"Do your duty in all things.... You cannot do more; you should never wish to do less." – Robert E. Lee

"The nation which forgets its defenders will itself be forgotten." – Calvin Coolidge

"I'm stronger because I had to be, I'm smarter because of my mistakes, happier because of the sadness I've known, and now wiser because I learned." – curiano.com

"A good plan, violently executed now, is better than a perfect plan next week." – George Patton, Jr.

"Stand up for something, even if it means standing alone. Because often times the one who flies solo has the strongest wings." – Unknown

"Be strong and courageous for the Lord will be with you wherever you go." – Joshua 1:9

"Be motivated by the fear of being average." – Unknown

"I do the best I know how, the very best I can, and I mean to keep on doing until the end." – Abraham Lincoln

"We are what we repeatedly do. Excellence then, is not an act, but a habit." – Aristotle

CALL TO ACTION

Supporting our veterans is of paramount importance. There is a great divide between what the government can provide in valuable resources to support transitioning veterans and what they need. This will take years to fix, with the state of the federal government and the lack of cooperation between political parties.

Our veterans are paying the price for this discord at a time when support is so critical, especially after years of war. A lack of resources has led to shocking results.

- Twenty veterans a day commit suicide.
- In 2014, 49,000 veterans were homeless. (The study is conducted every five years). This is eight percent of the total homeless population.

I'm personally heartbroken and disgusted by these statistics.

Our nation's commitment must shift. We must come together and bring all our resources to bear to support our veterans. They must know the resources available to them, and they must be able to access them easily. Most of all, our veterans must be assured beyond a doubt that we are a grateful nation, their duty and sacrifice are honored and valued, and their futures will deliver the rewards they so deeply deserve.

ABOUT DWAYNE D. PARO

Dwayne Paro served in the U.S. Air Force for eight years and supported the federal government for twenty years as a contractor in information technology. His commitment to and passion for supporting transitioning veterans led him to establish his veteran empowerment and transition practice to guide transitioning veterans to create and lead a fulfilling and empowering life that honors their duty and sacrifice. Over time, his support has expanded to an overarching focus on veteran empowerment which includes blogging, podcasting, the establishment of a mastermind group, and public speaking.

Dwayne's mission is to honorably and respectfully serve transitioning veterans and entrepreneurial veterans to persevere in defining and executing their future by providing an atmosphere of comradery and trust that honors their dedication and commitment. This will empower the veterans to feel whole, honored, respected and fulfilled in defining and living their life purpose.

Dwayne has been married to his wife, Melisa, for nineteen years. They are the parents of one son, Ty W-D Paro.

For more information and to work with Dwayne:

Dwayne D. Paro, Veterans Coach/Author/Blogger/Podcaster/Speaker

Landmark Life Coaching – Founder/Coach (www.landmarklifecoaching.com)

LinkedIn (https://www.linkedin.com/in/dwayne-paro-094848115/)

Charlie Mike Podcast – Founder/Host (www.charliemikepodcast.com)

Huffington Post - Guest Contributor (www. huffingtonpost.com/author/dwayne-paro)